# Super Crisis
## What in Earth is going on?

MARK V. STEINER

.

# DEDICATION

This work is dedicated to all medical professionals, doctors and scientists. Thank you for protecting our world, its development and prosperity with your work every day.

# SUPER CRISIS. WHAT ON EARTH IS GOING ON?

# DISCLAIMER

Although the author has made every effort to ensure that the information in this book was correct at press time, the author and publisher do not assume and hereby disclaim any liability to any party for any loss, damage, or disruption caused by errors or omissions, whether such errors or omissions result from negligence, accident, or any other cause. This work was prepared by the author in his personal capacity. The opinion expressed in this book is the author's own. The author and the publisher are not responsible for any errors or omissions obtained from the use of this information.

.

# CONTENTS

# ACKNOWLEDGMENTS

I want to thank my family for their help and support.

# 1 THE WORLD HAS STOPPED

The world has stopped; stopped waiting for tomorrow, waiting for the future, expecting that someone will say that we can live again like before. That everything is well.

The world stopped and allowed us to look around, think, ask ourselves important questions. What's happening? Why did this happen? What will happen next? If this is not the end of the world we lived before, then obviously it is its dress rehearsal.

When trouble came to everyone, it turned out that this is the problem of all humankind. And all of a sudden we became interested in what was in Wuhan, Italy and other countries, realizing that tomorrow trouble would come to our house. And it has happened. We see mobile morgues and empty streets worldwide. It is not the last epidemic, and certainly not the first one. But why was no one ready? What would happen if the virus was even more fatal?

The world has stopped. And for thousands of us, it has stopped forever despite the race, nationality, faith and depth of the pocket. It turned out that we are all the same.

Equally unprotected. And it became clear that we are all connected. The trouble in one part of the world will undoubtedly affect us all. We cannot close our eyes to the misfortune of another, even if it is overseas. It turned out that the words of doctors and scientists mean much more than political speech.

The world has stopped, and I ask myself the question: why this happened and what will happen tomorrow when we all go outside again and can get back altogether. After all, the pandemic turned out to be the trigger for a long-loaded weapon of mass destruction called the global crisis. There was no doubt that sooner or later, economic growth would slow down, and a recession would begin. But few expected the situation to take today's direction; that everything will happen so quickly and dramatically. The global coronavirus epidemic did not allow the economy to crawl to the finish line of growth but drove it headlong into the ground with a deadly knockout.

For some reason, only now, it has become apparent that vaccination is necessary, that the work of health workers on which our health and life depends is priceless. That scientists solve much more essential problems than it seemed before; that the survival of all humankind depends on professionals. It turned out that the world community can unite against a common enemy, and most of the everyday global problems could be resolved within a few months.

People begin to believe that it is possible to change the situation. This crisis has shown that the modern world is very vulnerable and that we are not able to confront real global threats. If this virus does not already teach humanity a lesson, then it is unlikely that a bright future or any future awaits us.

But what is happening today? And what awaits us tomorrow? In the sea of information that hit us every day, we wander like a small boat in a storm. We are not able to look at the whole situation from the outside, and see the light of a lighthouse behind another giant wave of fears. What is going on meanwhile in the depths is generally hidden from our eyes.

But if we try to analyze the current course of events, compare it with the previous experience of humanity and consider the fundamental processes occurring in principle and directly affecting the economy and society, the situation may become a little clearer. And it will become apparent in which direction the wind of change is blowing, where are we going and what awaits us when the storm subsides.

No one can reliably say what awaits us tomorrow. But, it becomes quite evident that after such global events, we will never be the same again. The world is changing dramatically. And I hope that we can all survive this super crisis. All of us, one way or another, must solve the accumulated global problems and take part in the construction of a new world. I would like to believe that a better world.

In the meantime, we are in the thick of things, let's put on life jackets and try to figure out what the hell is going on.

# 2 ECONOMY AND MONEY

Let's briefly plunge into history to get an idea of where we are now and how we got to this, and whether we had a choice.

Throughout human history, people created money many times. Their development did not require technological breakthroughs, but rather a revolution of the collective imagination since it implied the creation of a new reality that exists only in the human mind.

Money is not coins and banknotes, or even numbers on the screen. Money is absolutely everything that people agree to use for a systematic representation of the value of other things.

It all started with hunting and gathering, which prevailed over 90 per cent of modern human history. At that time, people were the jack of all trades. Weapons for hunting and protection tools, clothes, shoes, everything was created independently and exchanged at any suitable occasion. One thing changes to another without cash payment. In this case, one doesn't need money at all. For example, you have the skin of a recently killed mammoth, and your neighbour made a new axe for hunting. You need a new axe. The neighbour needs mammoth skin. Both of you agree on exchanging. Replace the skin and axe with any other goods, and you will get an idea of the exchange or barter system. Everything is straightforward. And that is why the system lasted a very long time.

But about 10,000 years ago, with the spread of people around the planet, the first plants and animals were domesticated. Agriculture appeared, the consequence of which was an increase in population density. At the same time, there was no need to create everything necessary for living independently. Instead, specialization appears: someone cultivated the land, others sewed, others baked bread. This specialization has created problems for the exchange system. The tailor could offer the farmer only clothes in exchange for wheat.

But the farmer does not need new clothes every day. And the tailor needs to eat every day. Therefore, it would be necessary to find another person who needed clothes and agreed to exchange for his goods. Which in turn, exchanged for food. There is a need to search for people who have what you need and are ready to trade it for what is in your excess. Some exchange game to get bread. In this case, it appears a need to introduce one rule for all to simplify the exchange procedure. And here the authority played an important role.

Let us look at the situation from a different angle. We can say that the introduction of money was promoted by natural human greed and a desire for dominance. Imagine yourself as the head of a small settlement. As a true ruler, would you be satisfied with what you already have? What kind of ruler are you if your ambitions do not go beyond your settlement? You want to reach out a little further.

You are a very successful leader, and you manage to organize an army of like-minded people. You are gaining power over the adjacent territories. They pay you tribute in the form of livestock or other goods. Your warriors are happy. You generously reward them with the received trophies. And now you are the great ruler of all the surrounding places. And yet you want more. You are about to go on a military campaign even further. And here, a problem arises. Your army needs food, equipment and weapons. Besides, warriors want to get paid for their risk. Since the campaign is distant, it is impossible to carry additional convoys with food or other products along with those necessary for the supply and vitality of the army. Paying meat and skins will be of little interest to anyone on the road since you will only be able to return home after months if at all.

Therefore, you need a solution. Something simple, compact, non-perishable and in limited quantities. The use of grain has a problem since you can grow more grain; the same goes for shells or pebbles. You can go to the beach and get rich. After all, how can one truly trust the currency system if anyone can create more currency at any time?

And you, as a wise ruler, introduce the Metal Money System. Unlike shells and grains, citizens could not just go and find more gold and silver and melt it into coins. Even in the modern world, despite the abundance of available tools, this is a rather specialized task.

Of course, at first, the population resist the innovation and does not understand how one small piece of metal can be the same as one cow or, for example, ten bags of grain. But over time, you manage to introduce the system everywhere. The system made it very easy to pay off the army and conduct long military campaigns. You also impose your idea on the conquered peoples and get a tribute from them precisely in metal money. Which makes much more sense, since the expanses of your conquests already extend very far from your village, and it is simply impossible to bring pay with food. Paying tribute with coins has become the norm. Now we take it for granted, but then these meal round discs were rather strange. Today, even paper money is becoming history. Now we believe in the value of the numbers on the screen, which became money.

Ease of use, the speed of the purchase-sale operation together with gaining more control over a large number of people are the eternal engines of new monetary systems. The money system proved to be the most effective in the struggle for survival. It allowed to become more powerful, conquer weaker ones, develop and strengthen states, impose the rules and tax the entire population.

The monetary system has consolidated and has survived more or less to the present day. The metal for coins had to either be obtained or taken from someone. Any attempt to become richer could be realized only at the expense of someone else. Since inside social conflicts weaken society and undermine power, each ruler strongly supported only external conflicts. The conquest of neighbouring tribes, peoples and countries, robbery of all uncontrollable were encouraged by the state because it brought money to society. Disputes within the community create difficulties for rallying and organizing the people. The myths that neighbouring tribes are entirely different people were often used, justifying the sacred matter to rob and kill them.

Moreover, the dissemination of the idea of self-restraint, self-sacrifice, tolerance, and the inevitability of fate become the most effective system for limiting conflict situations within society. Intolerance and punishment of dissent are encouraged. Obedience and humility within the community have taken for granted, following dogma promised a joyful existence not only in life but also beyond it. People who helped spread these beliefs enjoyed the particular favour of the state and even were exempted from taxes.

Imagine that you live in a medieval town and decide to open a butcher's shop to earn some money. In this town live 1000 people. Let's say the community consumes a thousand kg of meat per week. The population does not grow because of fatal diseases, wars, disasters, lack of hygiene and medicine. It is rather great luck if the community at least remains the same. In this situation, if you somehow managed to find yourself a few customers, all of them turn out to be former customers of another butcher of this town. He has been working in the city for a long time. And by taking his customers, you also take away his income. Of course, he would not like it. Having gathered all his relatives and friends, he would cheerfully go smashing your store. In turn, your family would begin to defend your new source of income. Such fights certainly disrupt the peaceful social life, which in any case has many problems.

Therefore, the authority with all their powers tries to prevent such events. In the medieval town, everyone went about their business and passed it from father to son, and so on. Therefore, we can meet many surnames such as Tailor, Steiner, Miller, Bauer, Mayer. These surnames indicate the type of activity that the family engaged in. It was usually not just difficult to change the line of business, but very unpromising. Let's say, despite all the difficulties, you still decided to open a butcher's shop in this town and take away the customers from the local butcher. But where do you get the money for the room, equipment and people? Who would invest in the project?

Let's take a closer look at the situation. Firstly, consumption and the amount of money in society does not change. The likelihood that you return the investment is minimal since the city already has its butcher. His business runs excellent, and everyone knows him. How do you plan to get clients? To attract someone to your shop, you need to reduce the price. Reduced price, in turn, lowers the profitability.

Moreover, nobody needs problems and conflicts in an established closed society. The authorities always try to unite the population in every possible way: common language, faith, beliefs. How can you stand shoulder to shoulder against a common enemy if you have a lot of conflicts within the community? What would happen if you turn your back to your busyness competitor on the battlefield? He will not miss the opportunity to get you out of business. Therefore, hardly anyone would invest your project in the Middle Ages.

One of the most famous and revealing stories about the problematic investment in medieval times is the expedition of Christopher Columbus. At one time, he proposed an incredibly profitable business idea - to put together an expedition to find a short way to India. This startup would bring colossal profitability and would return all investments in a short time. He addressed many wealthy people of that time, monarchs and their subjects. But everyone refused him. In the end, Columbus was able to find an investor in the person of the Spanish crown only ten years later.

For centuries, nothing has changed regarding the amount of money and consumption. To increase consumption, one would have to sell something extra—some product or service, in addition to what the population usually buys. But for people to buy something extra, they must have extra money for it. It is possible to save money by denying yourself what you usually bought or receive money from outside the system. The first option is unlikely because people purchased only the necessities of survival. The second case arose only during the wars. Generally speaking, for there to be more money, there must be an increase in consumption. And without an increase in consumption, there can be no extra money. It turns out a vicious circle, a dead end. Money, like the blood of an economy, nothing happens without it.

It would seem impossible to find additional money and increase consumption without receiving money from the outside. But this problem has been resolved. Today we live with a system of concepts that allows us to create wealth from nowhere. How did this become possible? What enabled to move consumption off the ground? Where did the extra money come from? How consumption and the economy began to progress? And more importantly, how money, which does not really exist, can affect the economy, induce the incredible development of humankind and, generally speaking, create the world in which we live today. Thanks to a new idea, the idea of Fractional-reserve banking, over the past three centuries, our world has changed more than in its entire previous history.

A prerequisite for partial reserve lending was the emergence of paper money. As early as the hundredth year BC, the Chinese invented paper and soon found a fascinating application for it. Gold is a very soft metal. Gold coins are quite easy to damage, so with constant use, they are often deformed. Instead of carrying metal coins, one could leave all valuables in a bank. The bank issued a certified paper receipt confirming the value of the items, that is, a banknote. Each banknote corresponded to a certain amount of gold.

For a long time, banks gave money at interest. But the gold in stock was not endless. It was not possible to credit as many people as possible to get even more profit. Suppose a bank has 1,000 gold coins in reserves; hence the bank physically cannot give more than 1,000 gold coins on credit. The situation changes dramatically with the introduction of banknotes. It became possible to circumvent this limitation.

Taking into account the low probability of the situation when the whole population comes for Gold simultaneously, European bankers realized that one could not only issue banknotes based on the number of reserves in the bank, but also a more significant number of them. Gold lay in the bank. And in pursuit of super-profit, banks decided to issue liabilities two-three and even ten times more than it was provided with Gold.

For example, if the bank has 1000 gold coins, you can loan the amount of paper money that is up to 10,000 gold coins. This is called Fractional-reserve banking. These 10,000 gold coins are only on paper in the form of a bank commitment. Thanks to this process, it became possible to credit the development of the economy, which was impossible before.

It would be quite challenging to convince the producer to create 50,000 pairs of shoes if consumption does not grow. If only 10,000 pairs have always been enough. But with the advent of additional money, consumption has begun to grow. Accordingly, it has become profitable for an entrepreneur to engage in technologies that would allow producing faster and cheaper. The development of a business becomes advantageous.

Development of the economy, boosted the creativity to find new, more efficient ways of production. People have started inventing new things. Additional money and consequent higher consumption provoked the extra motivation to develop, research, study, open new horizons. Prerequisites for scientific and technological progress appeared. People have come up with millions of different things that have changed our world, such as an internal combustion engine, aeroplanes, cinema, the Internet, achievements in the field of medicine, space, communication, roads, factories. All this appeared over the past three centuries, thanks to a new ideology.

Look at today's world. There is a sea of money around us. And there are no problems to finance absolutely any project. The only thing needed is to convince an investor that the project will be profitable. We live in incredible economic development time, compared to the Middle Ages and before.

However, since the amount of Gold in the bank remains constant, and paper obligations are printed more and more, their value decreases. Therefore, over time, it will be possible to buy fewer and fewer goods and services for the same amount of paper money. Reducing the value of banknotes raises the overall price level of products and services. This process is called inflation.

Moreover, at some point, the bank's loan obligations become more than the return on these obligations, which leads to an economic crisis.

But since the Fractional-reserve banking system allows society to develop and progress, one has to put up with these problems. Money supply stimulates consumption, resulting in the development of technology and production. Thus we have created the world in which we live today.

It would seem that everything should function flawlessly. But let's take a closer look. With the introduction of banknotes, Gold is accumulated and stored in central banks of states. Paper money is issued under these gold reserves. People know that at any moment they can go to the bank and exchange their banknotes for Gold.

But as we have said, the constantly growing money supply is needed for economic growth. When banknotes are tied to Gold, even with fractional-reserve banking system, the gold reserve must increase all the time to ensure the growth of the money supply.

The amount of gold in the world is limited. The main part of it has already been mined, which is about 170 thousand tons.

Approximately 2 thousand tons of gold are mined annually around the world. It turns out that no matter how we try, the volume of gold extracted grows very slowly by about a per cent per year.

But the world economy is developing quite dynamically, relatively speaking, five per cent growth per year. This increase is usually expressed in the total cost of all goods and services produced in the state or gross domestic product (GDP).

For the development of the economy in a single country, it is necessary to increase consumption, which requires more money. Therefore, when tying money to gold, the so-called gold standard, states always need more and more gold reserves to provide a continually increasing money supply.

In this case, the country must either extract a lot of gold or borrow it. The first case is not always possible. The second option drives the country more and more into debt. And it turns out that upon reaching a particular development of the economy, it is simply physically impossible to provide so much gold.

Therefore, today banknotes are not tied to gold. The US dollar became the most popular world currency. And its value is no longer determined by gold in reserve but based on several factors, one of which is the demand for the US dollar in the world. And frankly speaking, today payments are made using unsecured money created on the initiative of one country.

Unlinking the banknotes from the gold standard makes it possible to print as much money as needed. But the uncontrolled printing of money leads to massive inflation and undermine the country's economic stability. Therefore, the central bank of the state strictly controls the issue of banknotes. In the United States, this is a Federal Reserve System created in 1913.

It is the control of the central bank that does not allow the economy to collapse. It can manipulate the speed of development. It fastens the economy when it falls and slows it down when it grows too fast. Therefore, the overall development of the economy is wavelike and goes in cyclical.

Imagine an economic situation at the lowest level. That is, after the crisis. The situation is stable bad. At that time, to induce the economy growth, Banks provide cheap loans. People start borrowing money; business is expanding, unemployment is declining, investment and production are rising. Over time, this develops into a phase of prosperity, when production volumes exceed the pre-crisis level and stabilize. Unemployment is at a minimum level, salaries are rising, and the prices rise as well. Therefore, the central bank increasing the cost of loans to slow down inflation. Goods fill the market, consumer expectations decline. At some point, too much product is produced, and consumers cannot buy everything. There is a decline. Business slows down; the population has less free money to spend. Demand is declining.

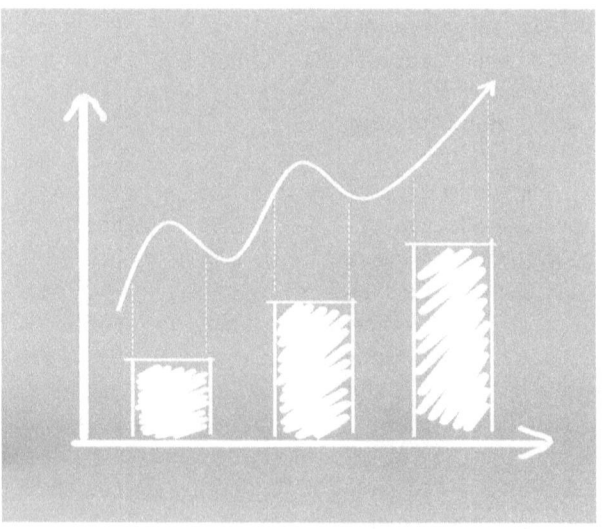

Unemployment begins to increase, as manufacturers reduce production. GDP growth begins to slow down, and the cost of loans reaches the maximum levels. The economy approaches the bottom phase of the cycle.

Goods are sold at a low price; trade is weak; the decline in production is slowing down; the unemployment rate remains high. In this phase, consumer expectations are very low. At this point, the cost of loans declines, which creates the prerequisites for the accumulation of capital. And the whole cycle starts from the beginning.

One can ask another question. If one can print as much money as needed, why not make all people equally rich (or equally poor) and divide the money evenly? If one tries to implement this idea, then after some time, a particular equilibrium state will be established in which most of the wealth will be concentrated in the hands of a smaller part of the population.

The world works on the principle of wealth redistribution. The means of production through which products and services are created belong to a small part of humankind. The production aims at making a profit for the investors. The actions are focused on the interests of a small part of the population. Another part of humankind in one way or another is employed or involved in the production. Let's have a closer look, what this setup can lead to without proper regulation?

Let's get closer to our time and imagine a particular country, where everything works good based on the conditions described above. Manufacturers receive large loans from banks and expand their production. The population is engaged in manufacturing and gets a good salary, which it then spends on buying goods and services in the local market. The owners of the production are satisfied, the investors are happy, and everything goes pretty well.

But at some point, the owner of the enterprise understands that it is possible to extract additional profit if the costs of producing goods are reduced. Hence, the production is transferred to a country where it requires less cost.

The products obtained in this case are still sold in our country. Income increases greatly. The owners of the enterprise and its investors are delighted. But what is happening in our country? People who previously worked in manufacturing companies were left without jobs since many production facilities were brought to countries with cheaper means of production. They must find another producer to get paid. However, most of the producers and owners of enterprises are guided by the same goal - the increase in profits. Therefore they do similar things to reduce production costs. The transfer of production leads to a rise in the number of low-income people in this country. People can no longer afford the goods that they got before.

The crisis is approaching. Those goods that were produced cheaply abroad must be sold in a given country. But demand is becoming limited due to the limited amount of money that people get. Most of the population in this market have become unemployed. They can no longer afford to buy as much as before when they had a well-paid job. Then the problems touch on the manufacturer and the investor. They made a product that they used to sell quickly at the local market. But now it is impossible because people without jobs don't have enough money. And people have no money because they lost their jobs when the production was transferred. The system devours itself. In pursuit of high earnings, lots of people are left without income.

Of course, the rules of market and competition are excellent things. But without proper regulation, this can lead to disastrous consequences. Numerous examples of our history show that rivers of blood were spilt in pursuit of profit. In a thirst for profit, people step over moral values. The mighty rulers colonized the weaker nations, sometimes oppressing and destroying millions of people. Slavers, arms, drug dealers, illegal prostitution, child labour - this is just a small list of what the world knows due to the people's greed. And here the authority plays a vital role as a controlling factor.

The state, as the political organization of society, monitors the order within this society. It also tends to protect the wealthy producers (capitalists) from the rest of the population, since they bring the major part of the money to the state treasury and give work to all the other inhabitants of the country. The magnitude of the influence and control of the state is a debatable topic, but the levers of influence on manufacturers must exist.

The state creates specific rules of the game for everyone, that is, institutions. These rules play a crucial role in the development of various spheres of human life. Political institutions are the rule of gaining and changing power, a system of checks and balances, protecting the rights of the majority and minorities.

Economic institutions are primarily the protection of property rights, the enforcement of contracts, and the protection of competition. Institutions also include an independent judicial system and a law enforcement system.

Indeed, one can come up with a lot of different rules, but if you look at existing historical experience, the most considerable economic development is observed in the countries, where the protection of property rights, an open political system, and strong judiciary systems are present. If there are no checks and balances in the political system, then it is difficult for the authorities to guarantee investors that their property will not be forcibly taken away by the state. In this situation, the incentive to invest is naturally much lower, which obviously has negative consequences for economic growth.

The colonized countries, in which the climate conditions were favourable, the long-term institutions were built based on the model of the metropolises. In these states, the institutions still work for economic growth and development, which made them prosperous countries today. They managed to build a developed society. AS an example, take a look at New Zealand and Australia.

Another example is institutions focused on extracting profit from the economy in the interest of a small elite. From the point of view of public consensus, this society has much less stability. And in most cases, economic growth is much slower than in the first case.

We can see that from world experience it is possible to get a lot of useful information, build theories and economic models. With the help of specific analytical tools, it is possible to describe and predict certain events in the world. But at the same time, the question arose: in the presence of so many economists, analysts and huge companies that predict market behaviour, why no one can determine precisely when the crisis will come. After the disaster in 2008, the Queen of Great Britain visited the London School of Economics. She asked economists how was it possible to miss the signs of approaching crisis. They answered that the main reason for the failure in predicting the financial crisis of 2008 was a lack of collective imagination among the brightest minds both in Great Britain and around the world. Does this mean that all the economists of the world simply missed the danger of the crisis? And why, then, to fund so many economists and analysts if they cannot predict such dramatic world events.

When we talk about the possibilities of predicting this or that event, we need to understand what economic science and science, in general, are. Science is associated with the repeated reproduction of the same results under the same conditions. Thus, for example, physics was built.

Galileo launched his ball through the gutter, measuring the time of its flight. And if today we repeat this experiment conducted 300 years ago, we will see that the result will be the same. And it turns out that if with the help of a specific set of knowledge, it is very likely to predict the outcome of an experiment conducted under identical initial conditions, then this system of knowledge could be called science.

Is it possible to conduct the same experiment in economics? The answer is simple - it is not. It is simply impossible. Let's imagine that in country A during a certain period, characterized by a certain set of parameters, there was hyperinflation. Today in country B there is a very similar situation, which presumably should give rise to the same effect.

But if we talk about repeatability, then it is entirely inadequate to compare these two situations, since we have only two observations.

No generalizing conclusions could be drawn, since it is necessary to repeat the situation (experiment) at least a hundred times to understand the causes and effects.

Practically such repeatability cannot be achieved. Only the most individual basic things, for example, how a person reacts to one or another price decisions can most likely be predicted based on observations on many people.

Today, economic science consists of many branches. It is very unlikely that in future, they all will be combined into one universal knowledge system. Different branches will be developed independently, and for each separate area, its own scientific instruments will be developed.

For example, there are auction theories, transport simulation theories; there is a theory of how people participate in elections. All of them are economic science. But it is crucial to understand that economics is a young science, and it has its strengths and weaknesses. The economy explores the behaviour of people as market participants and the collective expectation. It is not physics or chemistry. And it is impossible to predict how much the assets will worth, and how active are revalued, as it depends on what people think about the future of these assets.

It becomes clear that predictions in the economy do not always come true since the global social system is very complex and is subject to many unpredictable factors. But there may be some common features in past crises that can be used as pointers. Let's look at the most revealing stories of world crises, and try to find what we could use to describe the situation today.

# 3 WHAT AWAITS US? EXPERIENCE OF PREVIOUS WORLD CRISES

We all tend to think that in our life everything is very original and happens for the first time, but if you delve deeply into books and look at history, it will become clear that we are far from the first victims of such cataclysms. Disasters happened throughout all human history. Some of them were much worse, compared to what we see today.

Although economic crises are not entirely unpredictable, for most people, enterprises and entire countries, this event is a big surprise blow. Business goes bankrupt; people lose their jobs and savings. Tragic situations become part of life.

The economic crisis is a complex event that changes our understanding of the world. It changes the whole way of life. Even if it is far from a possibility of sure prediction, previous world experience has shown that sometimes it is possible to find something in common between crises.

And one can determine a similar chain of events that preceded them. So let's take a look at the first world experience of the economic crisis. Why did it all happen and what was the main reason for it.

# The first world economic crisis

Life in the 19th century was quite different from our life today. Banknotes could be exchanged for metal money, silver or gold, in a bank. The value of a currency was determined by the content of gold in it. At that time, commercial banks had the right to print their own banknotes, since in any case everything was connected to gold.

In the US at that time, progress was in full swing. The thirties of the XIX century begins the railway boom; it starts in the northeastern part of the United States. For ten years (1830-1840), the length of railways increased from 40

miles to 2755 miles. The development of this infrastructure was simply phenomenal. No one was going to slow down. The country was tangled up by a railroad web connecting more and more cities. With such a speed of development, the railway sector proved to be very attractive for investment. Not only the United States but also Germany, France and the United Kingdom are investing vast amounts of money in the US railway companies in anticipation of profits.

Shares of railway companies are continually growing in value. Ordinary citizens invest their last money in everything that was connected with the railways. Many, counting on the further development of infrastructure, travel west. They buy up land, in the hope that the railway will get to these places, and they could sell it at an exorbitant price. It was a crazy time. No one even thought about a possible pessimistic scenario. Banks issued tons of loans; foreign organizations have invested millions in the US economy. Everyone was just in the euphoria of development.

Moreover, in 1848, gold is found in California. The general optimistic mood now shoots up to heaven. Hundreds of thousands of gold hunters head to California. The gold rush begins. People realize that these conditions increase investment in railways.

Another critical point was the speed of information sharing in the mid-19th century. With telegraph development, it became possible to send information around the US within minutes. It took days and weeks before.

Meanwhile, in 1853, a war against the Russian Empire began in Europe. At that time, Russia was one of the world's major grain suppliers. In connection with the war,

Russia is reducing the supply of wheat and other grain for export. Worldwide demand for this product is increasing. In the wheat market, prices double. This fact added optimism to American farmers, who now quickly sold all available wheat abroad. Most of them took large loans to expand their land. All of America shook with a fever of money. Railroads were built at an incredible pace, gold was mined in huge quantities, and all grains were bought up at an attractive price. In such an atmosphere, it was tough to stand still and resist the temptation to increase profits. The constant increase in wheat price encouraged farmers to take more loans for new land.

But there is a limit to everything, and in 1856 the war in Europe ends. The Russian Empire returns to the list of international grain exporters, where it is one of the largest competitors to the US. The price of wheat is falling as supply becomes much more abundant. Farmers took huge loans in anticipation of their repayment, relying on the high demand. The decline in global need and lower wheat prices was the first problem in the house of cards that began to fall apart.

Banks, as one of the central players in any financial world event, were in the centre of the storm. The ratio of deposits and loans began to grow relative to the amount of gold stored in banks, which in this case indicates the growing risk of the banking system.

By 1857, more than 30 thousand miles of railroads had already been built, which is three times more than just seven years ago. Railways paid big dividends; their shares grew; the profits of almost all railways were above all expectations. This situation gave rise to firm confidence in the future performance and continued growth of stocks. Everyone tried to join the success of the railways' industry. People invested their last money in the furnace of a locomotive of the American economy rushing uphill, not thinking that it was approaching the edge of a cliff.

However, as it turned out, part of the railway companies existed only on paper without any funds for the construction of railways and rolling stock.

Some insurance companies were so carried away by the pursuit of increasing profits that they invested all available funds of investors in unsuccessful risky railway communication companies. It is not surprising that many companies lost the trust of investors, and in just five days, their capitalization decreased by 95%. This fact had woke up many investors from their sweet dreams.

Now they demanded payment of the invested funds, but companies and banks did not have enough money to pay back on the obligations that issued. Speculation with shares of railway companies and the land (remember those people who tried to buy the land where the railway will go) is rapidly depreciating. Depositors rushed to banks for the sole purpose of returning their invested funds. But that was already impossible. On one day, 175 banks abandoned their obligations. Another 150 Banks did the same in a week. Day after day, virtually the entire banking system was paralyzed. Trust in banks and their banknotes fell sharply.

The fall began on all fronts. People demanded funds back. Investors tried to stop their losses by selling shares and bonds of the railways. The sharp sale of stocks pushed prices down even more. Many farmers and industrialists who hope for future income became bankrupt.

The spread of the panic was also facilitated by the telegraph. Most of the territory of the US was covered by a telegraph web. News spread quickly throughout the country.

Another deadly hit to the economy was the wreck of a ship full of gold that was heading to New York to raise the level of money to local banks. About 400 passengers and 9 tons of gold drowned on September 9 due to a hurricane off the coast of North Carolina.

The American panic quickly spread to the UK, which was a major investor in the American economy.

British banks could not withstand the raid of excited citizens. People wanted their money back because of the sharp fall of American securities prices.

This crisis lasted just a couple of years but showed an example of a global economic collapse. Risky investments and unreasonable lending were the cause of the crisis as well as the rapid speed of information transfer, which increased the panic and influenced the course of events.

## The Great Depression

To date, it has been the most severe sudden and most famous global crisis, which is known as the Great Depression.

The crisis was so terrible that it not only bankrupted many banks, private households, and individuals but literally killed many people.

Before World War I, the United States was an agrarian country. The global military conflict largely triggered the growth of industrial production. Both sides of the conflict in Europe needed food and equipment. Under these conditions, the US became the leading international supplier, trading y successfully with Europe and continuously increasing production volumes.

Europe paid military debts in gold. The US treasury was replenished, production expanded. The US economy has been boosted; the whole country was electrified. Income from production began to multiply. The population employed in production spent lots of money on new gadgets like vacuum cleaners, refrigerators, radios. All that was previously available only to the rich people, today was in every household.

But as it is now, not all people could afford to buy everything they want on their own. Expensive goods required loans. The newly created US Federal Reserve System filled the economy with cheap money. A well-known formula has appeared "buy now pay later." This frivolous statement not to worry about tomorrow and live today has been strengthened for a decade.

Every American has the right to be rich. The belief

arose that everyone should have a car and their own home. Banks generously distributed loans secured by land and housing. Gradually, debt receipts fill the economy. It seemed the era of limitless prosperity began where everyone wanted to look and be successful. The more jeans you had, the bigger car you drove, the more successful you were considered. The consumption culture was born, which is living to this day.

The stock market was doing very well. In this increasingly positive trend, ordinary citizens also gain access to stocks, which are advertised everywhere. Each person gets a feeling that the stocks if something one should invest in. It becomes prestigious.

Unfortunately, people did not always buy stocks with their money. Very often, they carried out margin trading, that is, trading with the leverage of obtaining a loan for trading. Brokers in every possible way encouraged people to use a more considerable margin as a tool for earning more money. In this case, the risk is multiplied. It was possible to increase the winnings significantly exceeding the size of the collateral, but at the same time, the likelihood of a complete loss of money raised by several times if prices went down at least briefly. A tremendous amount of money from the real goods market spread to the stock market. It got to the point that 90% of all shares were purchased on borrowed money. Every 40 per cent of each dollar was spent on shares. A striking fact is that the government did not intervene in this mess. Bankers were able to convince the government that the market system is mature and autonomous, and therefore it is self-regulating and does not need the control.

Also, there was another factor inflating the financial

bubble to incredible proportions. There were many companies on the market that did not base their business on production. They got loans from banks and bought shares. And after some time they sold the shares profiting just from the growing value of securities. These companies successfully repeated this circle, thinking that this would continue forever.

But it was only an illusion. On October 24, 1929, people began to sell their shares. Millions of shares were sold, which provoked one of the most famous falls of the stock market. Nine billion dollars were lost within one day. It was the beginning of the end of general prosperity period.

It is worth mentioning that six months before these events, the biggest banks of the US exchange most of their assets into gold.

A half-year later, trying to stop a critical fall of the stock market, they began to buy up the shares of top companies. This tactic only helped for a few days. The fall resumed again. On October 28 and 29, the course of events took a tragic turn. Banks could not just issue as much money as needed since they were bound to gold. The fall of the economy has resumed.

The stock market crashed. People not involved in the investment process saw justice in this situation. After all, rich people lost money. Greed was punished. But the mood is changed just a few weeks. The salary was delayed; mass layoffs started in the companies and productions.

Unemployed people had to take their savings from the banks, where many kept almost all of their money. However, banks were not able to return the money. Since the state did not regulate the banking system, banks used the money for their own purposes. When the panic began, it turned out that the banks had insufficient assets that could be sold to return money to people. Banks declared bankruptcy due to lack of liquidity. People lost 25 billion personal savings, which amounted to a quarter of the country's GDP. The business could not continue working without bank loans and closed down. It brought a new portion of the unemployed. Every fourth person in the country lost the job. The state was not able to pay unemployment benefits to so many people at once.

At the same time, banks required payments on loans. People left without work, savings and state support, were unable to pay a mortgage on housing and millions of families ended up on the street.

Without bank loans, farmers also went bankrupt. At that time, the US was mainly a farming country. Hundreds of thousands of people engaged in farming provided bread not only their country but also half of Europe. The bankruptcy of banks in 1929, deprives farmers of money and their labour depreciates. The crop was left on the fields. Milk was poured on the streets. Many did not receive any income at all. They and their families were forced to go to the cities in the hope of finding jobs. The government has lost control of the situation. Famine began in the country. The streets in the cities were full of queuing for food people. Hunger riots appeared here and there. During the crisis, more than a million Americans died of starvation. The country plunged into complete chaos.

Millions of people were plunged into the horror of ruin, famine, lack of money. Their life has changed forever. A catastrophic situation paralyzed the economy, enterprises, people. The illusion of eternal prosperity perished overnight, making a colossal blow to the population. Successful people a month ago were ready to work just for food.

In this period of global shock, devalued and bankrupt state companies and private enterprises were bought by a particular circle of people for a penny.

Thousands of people not able to cope with the situation ended their lives by committing suicide. The number of suicides increased by 50 per cent after 1929. unemployment reaches 25 per cent. In the year the Great Depression began, the US produced 12 per cent fewer goods and services than the previous year; following years the situation got even worse - minus 16 per cent and minus 32 per cent of GDP accordingly.

On average, in 1920ies, about 70 banks were closed per year. In great depression time, in just ten months, 744 banks have closed. All together 9,000 banks went bankrupt; people received at best, only ten per cent of their invested money.

Only in 1933, the global fall of the market reaches the bottom. With the advent of the new president, Franklin Delano Roosevelt, a period of economic recovery begins. All banks were closed to stop the uncontrolled write-off of funds from deposits. State programs of economy support were launched.

Lots of people were hired for road repair or bridges construction work. At the same time, the state forcibly buys all gold from the population at a fixed price. In the event of a refusal to sell, a huge fine or imprisonment was imposed. Without gold, the only means of wealth accumulation was the American dollar. The government introduced the deposit insurance and government regulation of markets. The global construction of roads and bridges developed the new infrastructure and provided the prerequisites for further economic regeneration. The

US began to recover.

After the Great Depression, on the eve of World War II, many countries were in a deplorable state. The global crisis has affected the whole world. Britain's GDP fell by 23%, minus 24% in France, and minus 41% in Germany. It was the time when authoritarian and totalitarian regimes came to power. It was easy for them to point out the failed American capitalism and implement the new regimes, claiming that capitalism was not working.

## Crisis 2008

A significant driver of the US economic growth in the early 2000s was the construction sector. During this period, many Americans were able to get new housing. The mortgage market was growing rapidly. There was an opportunity to buy apartments under fairly acceptable conditions.

At the same time, the US Federal Reserve System reduces the rate on government bonds to one per cent. It meant that banks can now borrow money from the Federal Reserve System almost for free, which significantly spurred the US economy. Banks began to grow by leaps and bounds.

From the other side, for investors, 1 per cent of the yield was unattractive. They stopped buying Fed securities, looking for more profitable ways to invest.

And this way has been found. Banks got the idea to connect homeowners and investors through a mortgage.

A family sets aside part of their income for a down payment on a mortgage. A real estate agent connects the family with a bank, which gives the family a mortgage loan, that is, a loan secured by housing.

A bank tries to pack its mortgage portfolio into some kind of financial instrument called a derivative. Subsequently, a bank wants to sell this derivative to an investor or a larger bank. Rating agency evaluating the situation on the real estate market and the structure of the mortgage portfolio, of course, gives a good rating to the derivative, as a reliable financial instrument.

Banks earn in this way millions, investors have found a more successful way to invest their money. Families received housing. And everyone is happy. That is, banks and brokers managed to unite two groups of people - homeowners and investors.

At some point, the American mortgage market was already full of reliable borrowers. Therefore, banks began to check borrowers not so carefully. Moreover, mortgage conditions were so attractive that a person with a minimum income could get housing.

The first few years it was possible to pay only interest on the mortgage, and not pay the primary debt. Therefore a large percentage of the population was able to afford it. Even an unemployed person receiving benefits could pay interest on a mortgage. But not the primary debt.

However, in pursuit of even higher profits, the Banks continued to provide the derivatives based on mortgages, which already consisted not only of "good" loans but also of "bad" ones. These derivatives are sold on the market to investors who, of course, wanted to make money on the boom of the American real estate market.

But, as in the previous crisis, everything comes to an end. There comes a period when the borrower needs to pay not only the interest on the mortgage but also part of the primary debt, and now you need to pay monthly not just 200 or 300 dollars but ten times more. Many borrowers who easily received a mortgage were not able to do it. More and more housing were taken back by banks. Now there are a lot of free houses on the market, which causes supply growth with the same demand, which leads to the fact that prices not only slow down their growth but also fall sharply.

A lot of people could not pay their mortgages. Accordingly, banks were now unable to pay interest to their investors. The system began to collapse and caused a general fall in the American market, which affected absolutely the whole world. The financial system as a whole turns out to be frozen, and a wave of bankruptcies has begun.

# SUPER CRISIS. WHAT ON EARTH IS GOING ON?

# 4 UNSOLVED PROBLEMS

The recession of 2020 was expected. Lots of forecasts and predictions about the impending global crisis stemmed from the analysis of the current situation of the global economy. Unfortunately, no one could say that it would be such a global disaster—a real economic tsunami. Structural imbalance, as well as individual households` debts, interfered with the stable growth of the economy. American debt on loans set a new record, and the total debt of US residents to banks in the middle of 2019 reached a new historic high.

It is essential to note that the mortgage debt exceeded the 2008 historical level. The previous chapter showed the result of such a situation when real estate prices in the United States began to fall at an unprecedented rate. Banks collapsed, followed by mortgage companies. Since 2008, these systematic global problems have not been resolved.

Talking about Europe - since 2019, accepting deposits in euros was unprofitable for banks. World debt with a negative return of $ 14 trillion. It means that you give your money to a bank and it returns less money back. So, people who have bank deposits in euros will not even get what they deposited. It may seem absurd, but this is the situation in 2019. For more than a year now, the euro has been in the territory of negative interest rates, which destroys the financial system. At least 160 billion euros of savings were lost annually.

Central banks do not have any tools to counter the real economic crisis effectively. So, we see the apparent inconsistency of modern institutions in any way to control the situation, both nationally and globally.

The European Central Bank admitted in advance that the policy could provoke a stock market crash, confirming that low rates can support the economy, but free money encourages investors to make increasingly risky investments. Even financial market players such as pension funds and insurance companies take on too much risk by investing in unsecured assets.

Many pensioners who rely on their savings in the United States of America and Europe may be left with nothing. The same considerations apply to people with insurance.

Many companies that invested in a risky market segment may get rid of the assets in a hurry, which will provoke a stock market crash. The whole class of poor workers has formed in the World. In the US alone, 10 per cent of American households own 84 per cent of all stocks. It is a massive stratification in society. All the remaining 90 per cent of Americans own only 16 per cent of the stocks. So, economic growth makes the rich even richer, and the poor become only poorer. So, only 10 per cent of society benefits.

In the 60s, the robust lending to American households led to fast economic development, followed by the collapse in 2000. After which the recovery took place. But again, loans were issued to those who could not afford them, which ended up in the crisis of 2008.

Analysts have indicated that the cyclical crisis is on the verge. It was expected. So what have governments done in most countries around the World? How did they respond to existing problems? Have any attempts been made to fundamentally change the system to prevent or at least smooth out possible consequences in the future?

The global environmental situation escalated the crisis. We are talking not only about nature, irreversible loss of resources but also about human survival in general.

Experts estimate that as a result of irrational land use, humankind has already lost 2 billion hectares of once productive lands. It is more than the entire modern farming land area. Annually, as a result of soil degradation, up to 15 million hectares of fertile land are gone from the world agricultural turnover. They turn into deserts or used for constructions. At such rates of degradation, the productive soil may soon be completely depleted.

The concentration of chemicals in the surface waters changes dramatically. This most valuable renewable resource in the loop of the biocenosis has ceased to be restored to its previous natural form, having passed into the category of non-renewable resources. Some regions of the planet have already encountered a shortage of drinking water and are forced to impose strict regulations.

By 2050 the World's reserves of freshwater may be reduced by two-thirds. Just imagine how valuable the remaining third will be. Nature is immersed in the products of human life. One resident of the European Union, on average, produces half a ton of garbage per year. At the same time, countries such as Sweden and Switzerland recycle all their waste. The entire population is involved in the recycling process. But if some countries have found a solution, why the rest of the World is sinking in the sea of waste?

Up to date, humans have successfully destroyed the ecosystem of most of the land. The animal and plant variety is shrinking at an incredible speed. The amount of fish in the oceans is dropping. The catastrophic decline in the population and the complete disappearance of valuable species of fish and other marine inhabitants is the clearest example of a person's readiness to exploit the planet's natural resources until they are entirely extinct. Men turned out to be so stupid that they forgot that the resources necessary to support their life are developed within the framework of interconnected ecosystems. The production of oxygen, the natural filtration of water, the circulation of nutrients, pollination - all this is the result of a complex mechanism of living nature, in which man himself is just one of the equal links.

The systematic destruction of forests around the World has been going on since the beginning of the colonization era. Civilization was making its way, rapidly exploring new territories for cities, agricultural land and pastures. By destroying forests, we are destroying the vital habitat of plants and animals. As a result, there is a loss of biological diversity, a threat to the existence of the most important ecosystems, and an increase in the greenhouse effect due to a catastrophic decrease in the volume of photosynthesis.

Besides, many factors are affecting the Earth's ecosystem, and are not that obvious at first glance. We have a vague idea of the Earths' inner structure. Many facts are indicating that the Earth is warming up, but no one can explicitly explain why. An even greater mystery and the threat of climate instability. The mathematical models created today cannot explain these fluctuations. Over the past ten years, the polar regions have lost 15 per cent of the ice cover. Unprecedentedly hot summers in Europe have been observed in recent years. The fires in Siberia and Australia only in 2019 destroyed a vast number of forests and caused disastrous damage to nature.

Temperature increase on the planet by only 3-4 degrees will lead to simultaneous melting of ice in Greenland, Arctic and Antarctic. This situation would decrease the temperature of the oceans, which may affect the temperature of the Gulf Stream and the entire Earth's climate.

If the sea level rises, many megapolises will go

underwater.

Many populated territories will be unsuitable for living even before they are flooded. The combination of humidity and heat will make life impossible. This will entail a disaster for more than 2 billion people who will be forced to move inland.

A migration of billions of people to new territories would create a unique critical situation. We have seen the effects of migration from Syria. Only a few million refugees had a significant impact throughout Europe. Moreover, the smaller living space increases the additional tension in society. The proof of this is the history of the 20th century. The number of people on the planet increased from 2 to 7 billion, and during the same period, there were the bloodiest wars in the history: the first and the second world wars, the war in Vietnam, the Arab-Israeli conflict, the war in Afghanistan. The demographic situation in the World is heating up. Such regions as Africa and South Asia show tremendous population growth rates.

According to forecasts, the population of Africa will

double in the next 25 years. Even though life in these regions is incredibly complicated, it can be aggravated by climate problems. Then global migration will lead to a complete global collapse.

Natural processes of self-regulation of populations also apply to humans. If the population increases, there is a need for a corresponding increase in the resources necessary for existence. Their shortage increases mortality and, accordingly, the population size decreases. The amount of food is the most apparent factor that prevents living organisms from indefinite multiplication.

Whenever new ways of food production were invented, the World's population also multiplied. Once people mastered the hunt for big animals, the first demographic boom occurred. Then agriculture provoked a second population jump. The third demographic increase has started a hundred years ago and continues to this day. It is associated with the invention of fertilizers and genetic engineering. Nevertheless, the World's population is growing one and a half times faster than food production. Thirty-five billion people is a critical population of the Earth, behind which the global starvation starts.

Moreover, the world of technology has progressed so much that the human himself becomes redundant. We found ourselves in a situation where the population is needed only as a consumer. Robotic production displaces all manual labour. Systems based on Artificial Intelligence solve problems faster, cheaper and better. In many industries, there is even no light and heating. Robots work there 24 hours a day, seven days a week, and 365 days a year. They do not get tired, do not sleep; they do not need to pay sick leave or insurance. They do not complain about poor working conditions. The only thing they need is energy.

And this is another global problem of modern world society, unsolved until 2020, which will be addressed during the super crisis. Energy can be obtained from many sources and converted into the form required by the consumer. The difficulty is not the lack of energy. The problem is its profitability, as the ratio of the ready-to-use energy to the energy required to produce it.

Since the mid-sixties, the economic profitability of oil has been declining. Oil and gas supplies are enough for many more years. The problem is that it is getting more difficult to extract. The production difficulties require more and more energy. The renewable energy sources, like the energy of the sun and wind, are still far away from being competitive to fossil fuels. It is impossible to satisfy the worlds energy needs with windmills and solar panels. Nuclear energy is artificially restricted due to activists' protests, especially in Western Europe. A decrease in energy profitability naturally forces the population to every way motivating to reduce consumption. Consume less and work more.

The world is on the verge of tremendous change. The unsolved global problems that have accumulated for decades have formed a critical mass. And this time, everything went completely different. The pandemic that came to us so suddenly swept the whole world, made us look at everything differently, and revealed all these problems in the context. Hopefully, they will be resolved and not postponed until the time when we find ourselves in a hopeless situation.

# 5 FACING THE COLLAPSE

Due to the cyclical nature of the economy, a slowdown in its growth is an entirely normal phenomenon.
In 2019, all the largest economies in Europe, if they were not in recession, were on the verge. But for the onset of the global crisis, the problems of European countries are not enough. In 2019 China, as the second economy in the world, showed the lowest GDP growth in 28 years. Only the United States still showed strong economic growth. Moreover, the US economy broke the record for the most extended period of prosperity in history - 121 months without economic crises.

The current phase of prosperity turned out to be the longest, but rather slow in terms of GDP growth - 25 per cent in one hundred and twenty-one months. Additionally. The situation was heated up due to the United States and China Trade War and the Brexit process (the official exit of the UK out of the European Union).

The whole world was preparing for a smooth slowdown in the economy, trying to stimulate it by lowering rates. Given the availability of cheap loans, people are buying, business and production are expanding. In today's system, consumption is at the centre of development and progress. The whole economy represents the sum of all transactions between people. After all, every dollar you spend is someone else's earnings. Spending stimulates the economy. But in the previous year, world experts noticed that people begin to spend less, determining the beginning of a projected slowdown in economic growth.

Yet, with the impact of an unpredictable global event, the expected recession can develop into an unforeseen depression.

For all previous crises, people still had an opportunity to go outside to participate in the market. Now there is a problem with leaving the house. Economic activity has stopped. People just cannot come to the place of transactions. Previously, restaurants closed due to a decrease in the number of visitors. Now the number of visitors is zero. It means that the waiter could be fired. Without a job he will save money on the hairdresser, the hairdresser will not go to the fitness centre, the employee of the fitness centre will buy less food at the supermarket. And all of them will not go on vacation this year. The whole economy has been artificially frozen.

Today we live in an unprecedented situation when an unpredictable global event has occurred and affected the whole World. Many financiers knew that a recession comes. But the case when everything will happen so unexpectedly and abruptly, no one could have imagined. The whole World stopped in shock from what was happening. The expected economic downturn is turning into a free fall. And the speed of this economic decline depends on timely action by the government. Unprecedented measures have been already taken today in each country.

In the US the situation has changed so dramatically, that the bankers had nowhere to go, they began to do what the government requires from them. A tremendous amount of money supply is being issued to at least somehow slow down the decline. The US government managed to consolidate the Treasury and the US Federal Reserve under its management to finance private companies. To some extent, the state becomes the owner of these companies, and some kind of nationalization is taking place. In this case, there is a shift from capitalism to socialism, because the main key feature of socialism is that the means of production do not belong to the capitalists, but to all the people represented by the state. What will come of this, we will see shortly.

.

# 6 WORLD PANDEMIC AS A TRIGGER OF SUPER CRISIS

For many of us, it is obvious what exactly triggered the crisis that we are facing today. The global coronavirus epidemic has made us all see the world from a completely different angle. The world is different today - masks on the faces, closed borders, empty streets, crowded hospitals, mobile morgues, hundreds of thousands of dead.

COVID-19 kills. It does not ask what social status or income one has. It does not choose. We are informed about the significant number of deaths daily. But in a few years, when and if we look at the real statistics, everything will look much more severe.

On November 17, 2019, the first patient with coronavirus was registered in Wuhan, China. Only after two months, the quarantine started. During this time, the coronavirus could spread to a vast number of people both in Wuhan and throughout China. Later it freely moved to Europe, where it caused the effect of an exploding biological bomb. We are experiencing an unprecedented pandemic. A considerable number of people turned out to be infected. The entire world economy falls to the most profound and most severe economic crisis, with all the dramatic consequences.

Have all possible measures been taken to stop the epidemic when it was possible? Is this situation happening for the first time, and neither the national authorities nor the world community could do anything? Why information about the virus, the diseased, the course of the disease was not promptly shared with the relevant international organizations, to, if not prevent, then at least prepare for the impending danger. What has the World Health Organization done to stop the epidemic in the bud exactly where it originated? Indeed, a timely response is the main success factor in anti-epidemic measures.

In 2003, an Italian doctor, Carlo Urbani, who travelled to Vietnam due to an outbreak of an unknown disease, promptly identified a new and hazardous infectious disease (Severe Acute Respiratory Syndrome (SARS)). He immediately ordered the use of masks and protective clothing to all medical personnel, gave strict instructions to the Vietnamese government, demanded the introduction of quarantine and anti-epidemic measures. Thanks to his early warning, it was possible to localize the epidemic and organize effective countermeasures in time, presumably saving millions of human lives. One person was able to divert the greatest pandemic and incredible economic collapse from the world.

COVID-19 kills. But the extent of its action is different in different countries, which is the subject of intense attention and study. Specialists will analyze it for a long time to come. Why are infection rates, prevalence, and mortality rates so different in different countries?

Today there is no country in the World, where the number of hospital beds, medical professionals and essential equipment is enough to cope with the situation without implementing quarantine actions.

If the situation with the virus happened 20-30 years ago, no one would pay as much attention to it as we have it today. Everyone would wear a protective mask. The media would report that it is necessary to be careful. But no one would have thought that everyone would need to isolate himself, keep social distance, close the national borders, stop the economy.

The Internet has completely changed the scale and level of humanism throughout the World. The value of human life and human health has grown. Now the unspoken social agreement is such that it is possible to some extend sacrifice the economy for the sake of human lives.

Based on the following considerations, most countries introduced a quarantine. The strictness of quarantine directly depends on the balance of potentially seriously ill patients and the maximum capacity of the healthcare system. It should be able to accept patients and help, not exceeding the permissible risk to which medical personnel are exposed. So, the balance between the maximum number of seriously ill patients and the ability to help them, in which the health care system will have to continue to work smoothly and does not collapse.

If the health care system can help, for example, 200 seriously ill patients every day, then the quarantine measures should restrict the number of ill people to 200 at any given time. In this case, the epidemic is prolonged for a more extended period, compared to the situation if there was no quarantine implemented. It could be a year of slowly running epidemy compared to several weeks and 10,000 people ill at once. The epidemic does not last for five days if everyone who can get sick is sick. Let's say 10,000 people. And for a year. In this case, it becomes possible to save all those who could potentially die.

Sooner or later, everyone will get infected with COVID-19, and the so-called collective immunity will be developed. All quarantine measures are aimed at ensuring that there is no surge in the disease and, accordingly, protect the health care system from excessive load. That is what happened in Italy and China. In this case, the task of everyone is to get the virus, but as late as possible, when collective immunity already develops, the virus is not so aggressive, and not with such lethal consequences.

Unfortunately, in most cases, the quarantine plan for each country will not be determined based on the reports of virologists but based on political expediency. A government cannot stand and watch thousands of people die. On the other hand, a country cannot exist for a long time in a frozen state. On quarantine, people do not work, productions and business are stopped. Budget revenues are critically reduced. At the same time, money is being paid to people who are left without work, to support businesses, to emergency measures, to introduce and maintain quarantine, and treat a vast number of patients.

Three possible scenarios for ending pandemic are

possible.

The first scenario involves the development of a vaccine. It is crucial to make it clear that mostly, people die from the effects of coronavirus, a life-threatening inflammatory lesion of the lungs. And the vaccine that will be developed against COVID-19 will protect not from the coronavirus itself, but its consequences. And COVID-19 is likely to become a seasonal disease of humanity. Now the vaccine is being developed so that people who are age-related or weakened or with chronic diseases do not die but can overcome the virus without complications.

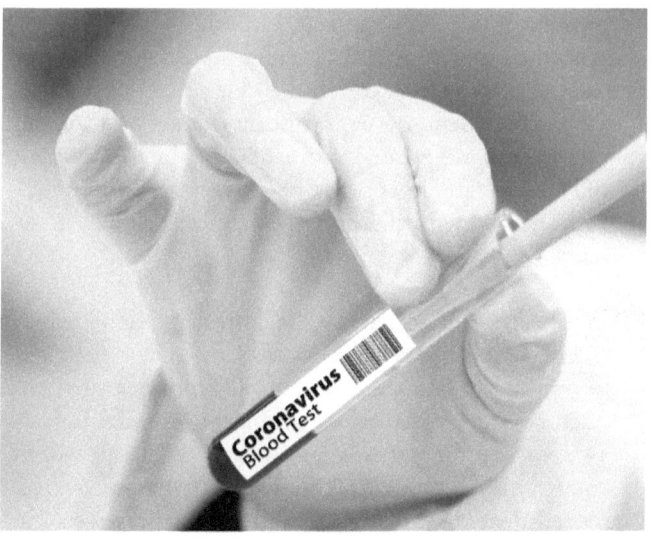

High level of science and technology today, makes it possible to develop the vaccine—currently, researchers all over the World working on it. There might be already many test vaccine against COVID 19, which will be used in the future if they pass a series of tests. And the main problem is precisely in these tests.

With the known genetic structure of a virus, researchers

looking for a substance that will effectively work against it.

The search can take a long time, and it is not always possible to get an effective drug at the first trial. Anyways, after this work is completed, it is necessary to test the substance. No one checks the cure immediately on people. First, tests are carried out on animals - on mice, dogs, then on monkeys. And if all the tests on three or better four animals pass successfully, only in this case clinical trials on volunteers begin.

It's important to understand that at any of the described stages, an error may occur, some side effects or complications may appear. In this case, the whole procedure starts over. On average, vaccine development takes seven to ten years. In the case of COVID-19, due to the involvement of a significant research resource, the vaccine can be created more quickly. In the best case, it will take at least one-two years. Based on the abovementioned, this option is applicable only in several years.

The second scenario. The introduction of quarantine will make it be possible to localize and defeat the virus. Let us imagine a situation where all countries are isolated. Each country would try to get back to normal functioning as soon as the virus is no longer a threat within the country. Everyone who could recover has recovered. No more infected, strolling freely through the streets. Such a country opens borders, and the virus can be again brought from the outside. The epidemic will recur in this case.

Moreover, in many countries, it is not possible to achieve complete isolation. There is no control over keeping people in quarantine at home; there is no sufficient awareness among people. In some cases, people cannot afford not to work, as their survival depends on daily work. That is, this option will work only if the whole

World is quarantined. Each country individually will defeat the virus within its borders, and the borders are closed until all countries are free from the epidemic.

Countries where the economic situation was difficult without the pandemic, would end up with the population having no savings after the first month of quarantine. Without means of living, society would be forced to terminate the quarantine, violating government orders. People will come out of their houses, and the infection will most likely spread further, killing an unprotected part of the population. And this is the third scenario. It is very likely that during a pandemic, most of the World's population will become infected with a coronavirus. People with strong immune system will suffer a coronavirus infection without consequences. Those with weak immunity are at high risk. They most likely will need medical help. Unfortunately, some of the patients will not be able to overcome the virus.

Whatever option is implemented, everyone must take care of their safety. But very often, when people take care of personal survival, they forget about common problems, get into depression and panic, which very often could be much worse than any pandemic.

It leads to chaos, violence and sacrifice. The situation is so unstable that state control is necessary.

To recall the empty supermarket shelves at the beginning of the quarantine - no toilet paper, cereals and canned food. Panic is much stronger than common sense. To understand how close we were to the wave of violence, imagine the following situation.

The first wave of panic occurs at any global event, that does not necessarily concern you directly. Understanding that the World is interconnected, you come to the supermarket to buy rice\pasta\toilet paper\any other product that you usually buy. Just in case, you buy an additional pack. Everyone else around is doing the same thing. Due to this unplanned demand, the stock of products is decreasing in warehouses.

If at this point, authorities do not introduce any restrictive measures, the situation goes on to the second wave of panic. You come to the store, and you see that the manufacturer slightly raised the price of the goods that you bought the day before. Now you are buying not two, but three packs of a product. And all the rest act accordingly. The manufacturer's stocks begin to disappear, because of unplanned increased and so high demand—disruptions in the delivery of products to the store started.

There comes the third wave of panic. You come to the store and see that there is simply no product on the shelves. And you buy another product to replace your need, even if you have never bought it before. And so not only rice, pasta and canned food but also other products disappear from the shelves of the store.

The fourth wave of panic comes. Warehouses no

longer have stocks of products. People buy absolutely everything that remains on the shelves, no matter what it is, which makes the store completely empty.

This is the fifth wave of panic. People come to an empty store and start violent behaviour since they cannot buy any food. The wave of violence and panic grows and spreads around the town.

The time needed to reach the last wave of panic is as little as ten days.

The authorities must always be with people in such situations. The task is to conduct outreach, prevent panic and chaos, limit provoked demand, protect the most vulnerable part of society. Especially during a pandemic when the economic situation is critical; markets collapsed, and it is not clear what will happen next.

We are witnessing a global super crisis. In the United States alone, more than three million applications for benefits due to loss of job were filed in just a week. According to the statement of the head of the International Monetary Fund, 80 countries have already applied for financial support.

Some media have declared a hope for a quick economic recovery immediately after the epidemic declines. Over the next six months, people will go to work, start buying in stores and travel; the market will expand, and the economy will actively work again. It is a somewhat optimistic forecast. And if quarantine lasts more than two-three months, then one should not expect a positive development of events in the coming years. Moreover, there is a high probability of getting a second wave of the epidemic in the fall of 2020.

Many specialized publications indicate that we are not just in a recession, but are rapidly plunging into a deep crisis, comparable to the great depression. The dynamics of the situation suggests that everything is much more severe than we think.

During the great depression, everything happened much more slowly than today. Only two years after the onset of the great depression, the unemployment rate reached 24 per cent. Now, in connection with the pandemic, this unemployment rate in the United States could be reached in just a few weeks.

The American stock market collapsed much faster than it was in 2008. Since the beginning of the great depression, the stock market has been falling for several years, but never as quickly as it is now.

Many analysts say that today, we have every chance of getting unemployment at 30 per cent, and a 40 per cent reduction in Gross domestic product. These are terrifying figures that indicate that the situation is very tragic.

People cannot be left alone face to face with the crisis. There is always someone who would offer society a radical solution to all problems. Nobody wants another global tragedy to happen. Therefore, the US authorities and other countries of the World fill the markets with money. In the long run, it will result in tremendous inflation, huge holes in state budgets, and the emergence of a large number of people who will live on benefits alone. But in the light of the consequences of the Great Depression, perhaps this will be the least evil.

# 7 A NEW WORLD

Today we experience a severe crisis that the world community will never forget. The economy suffers much, but there is still hope for a relatively quick recovery. The fact that everything happened so quickly and so unexpectedly is terrifying. The world was closed for quarantine. The consequences for the global economy will be eliminated for more than one year. But the most important thing is that everyone should learn lessons from the whole situation.

The artificially limited consumption will not come back by itself soon. After finishing quarantine, there will be practically no demand, a business will have to start all from scratch, and the massive unemployment will critically escalate the situation. Many developing countries faced a crisis without any financial reserves, and with substantial external debt. For them, this situation is much worse than for developed countries. Organizations such as the International Monetary Fund and the World Bank may now have a chance to help developing countries. Their reputation may improve soon. But how the situation will develop is still not clear.

Adjustment of world economic policy is needed. The countries with a high level of income and a developed financial system are better prepared for such a crisis. This is the United States, Western Europe, and Asian democracies. China coped with the crisis quite quickly. But it was in China that the local epidemic grew into a world pandemic. Information about what was happening was classified; there was no way to find out what was happening. Accordingly, crucial measures were not taken.

The success of the Scandinavian economic model in combating the previous crisis, as well as in the current situation with the epidemic, showed that it is essential to remember not only economic growth but also the fair distribution of benefits. Focusing only on economic growth, the UK and especially the US are strategically inferior to northern Europe.

Today there is already a revision of approaches to

economic policy. The pandemic has put the traditional US banking system in a difficult situation. The United States continues to issue money, which may save the declining economy at the moment, but in the long run will raise inflation to heaven. But since not only ordinary people and large companies need money, but also the rest of the business, the US banks found the same ground with the government. Although federal law explicitly prohibits Federal Reserve System financing of private companies, it was possible to find a technical solution so that the central bank of the US could buy up the debts of private companies in favour of the government. Today we observe the policy of an anti-globalization and an attempt to return strategic industries from Asia to the United States is in action.

The current crisis has also shown that in many countries, there is an institutional management crisis present. A challenge between civil society and the state woke up people and made them realize that they could not trust their government, which, under cover of a pandemic and crisis, decides its interests, while people locked in quarantine, are losing their jobs, retirement savings, and business.

A critical question from citizens to the state arises: who are you, the government? Maybe politicians are just people who got power in their hands? The so-called club of omnipotence, which is useless when real challenges arise. The doubts may appear that the state takes on too many powers during the crisis, but during an epidemic, state intervention is necessary.

The authorities exist to provide public goods. And the fight against epidemics is one example of what the state is for.

At the same time, we are witnessing the most tragic loss of human freedom. In a situation where people are frightened, the rights of the state are unhindered; the new restrictions are introduced for the person. It is important that after this crisis, society fights for the return of rights and freedoms because many states will not want to give them back. The community will have to unite and struggle for their old liberties. After all, it is a man who is the primary value for which the state exists. Therefore, it is a person, being a citizen, must demand that the state respects his rights.

Today we see that the system existing to this day is imperfect. No one can say for sure how all this will end, but the changes that are happening today in the social, financial and political spheres are tremendous. The world will never be the same as it was before. This may result in the new world order, anti-globalization, the end of the way of life that we all are used to.

The pandemic will leave a mark on our consciousness, perception of the world and interpersonal relationships for a long time. The rudiments of isolation, emotional loneliness and the crisis of social relations have long been laid down by the era of information technology and social networks.

With the advent of the pandemic, the estrangement of people one from another increased many times over.

All as if on command accepted the need for long-term self-isolation and limited communication. Now a stranger began to be perceived primarily as a personal threat. Just compare the reaction of people to any hint of illness a year ago and now.

Pandemics forced us to limit our daily emotional manifestations, shaking hands, touching, hugs, kisses.

Everyone who violates our personal space is perceived as a threat.

This new behaviour will stay with us for a long time. The scary image associated with the pandemic is now our daily routine. It would be nice to hope that someone announces soon that the pandemic is over, and we can live our lives like before. And forget everything associated with the virus, like a bad dream. But it is more likely, that after another wave of the epidemic, part of quarantine behaviour will stay with us forever.

The concept of work from home is already changed. In the nearby future, we will see even more remote work, online conferences, online process management. Much more productions will be possible to monitor and control remotely, projecting the actions on robotic installations while sitting at home. More automation, robotics and computerization are to come. Now replacing a person with a robot and artificial intelligence will not cause any objections. It will be taken for granted.

Closed national borders sooner or later will be opened. However, the crossing the border regulations will be already different and more strict. It will undoubtedly include checking the record of the person and, to some extent, medical control.

These restrictions, which would seem redundant recently, will now be accepted by the majority as necessary.

Justified by bio-security, freedom of movement will be significantly limited. The rules for obtaining the residence and work permits for foreigners might include new criteria.

Although the trend to listen to professionals, scientists

and doctors, instead of amateurs and charlatans, seams to be temporary, it gives hope to humankind for a better future. It turned out that vaccination is essential. And now people have more faith in science and pray from home for the fast creation of medicine, and the health of doctors.

Many people suddenly engaged in self-education. They read books, get acquainted with viruses and microbiology.

The understanding that one should not blindly rely on the state appeared. It turned out that in the face of real threats, the self-organization of society very often works much more efficiently than governmental regulations.

It is possible that with the forced isolation of countries, the policies aimed at solving internal problems will dominate over international trade wars and real wars. Everyone sees clear now that the World is small and very interconnected. It became evident that it is necessary to speak with each other, and it is possible to find common ground, especially at the face of a global threat.

The global situation requires a different approach to conflicts solving. There is a need to end wars and get out of crises peacefully because even bad peace is always better than the best war. But there is still a long way to a happy, peaceful life for everyone. The profit from the weapon trade is too high to stop conflicts. Moreover, gigantic military budgets need some reason to be justified.

Globalization has gone too far and carries high risks. The pandemic showed that each country should have a strategic supply of protective masks, medical equipment, chemicals needed for the production of certain drugs. Now everyone sees the importance of the modern health care system. The countries that have a developed health care system showed better readiness for such a pandemic. Nevertheless, the medical system also requires fundamental changes.

The concept of medical assistance should be reviewed; the remote medical help and self-assistance with home blood test systems should be widely introduced. A person should receive the necessary help without having to visit a doctor. All standard procedures, and those that can be done remotely from the medical institution, should be carried out at the patient's house, to protect the patients themselves, the medical staff. The hospital should be a place for emergency care, not a high-risk centre of disease spreading.

Nature recovers at an incredible speed. We involuntarily witness an astonishing experiment - a big part of World's population is locked at their homes, many productions are stopped, planes do not fly, there are fewer cars on the streets. It seems like we got back in time to an era when the World was not yet industrial.

Nature rests. Now everyone can see how much we influence the environment. Many of the plants, factories, and industrial facilities that emit nitrogen dioxide were suspended. Satellite images before and during the quarantine show that the level of air pollution in many industrial regions decreased by 25 per cent. The air in the cities has become much cleaner. Wild animals go to cities all over the World. Seismic noise from transport is significantly reduced, which has a positive effect on human health.

Our planet today seemed to have a holiday and time to refresh. Nature shows us what would happen if we at least sometimes stop and think about it.

Central banks are issuing more and more banknotes. The most significant change during the crisis is in their redistribution. Money changes their usual flow directions. If one money channel has dried up, then another one is filled up. Therefore, you do not need to wait until everything settles down, and the economy is in its lowest phase. Right now is the time to act. Watch for changes in the World, learn new things, and adapt accordingly.

Save money, do not invest impulsively. Take profits. Try to enter the market at the lowest prices. Develop your long-term strategy, be flexible and look for opportunities depending on the situation. Then there will be an opportunity not only to survive in such a difficult time but also to increase the wealth. But this is an entirely different story.

# 8 EPILOGUE

In the stream of apocalyptic information pouring out on us daily, everyone begins to worry about their life. But at the quarantine, it becomes clear that most likely we will all die not from the virus, but a disregard for each other. One of the most important discoveries for everyone is that we do not live alone. We have husbands, wives, children. Forced time spent together has opened our eyes. In many countries, there has been a surge in quarrels and divorces. Many people turned out to be completely unable to live together.

Many realized that they needed to work not only 8 hours a day at work, but also make efforts to work for their family relationships. Because family and close relationships are the foundation on which the rest of life is built. Healthy family relationships determine the ability to survive during hard times. I would like to ask each of you personally to remember this and pay attention to those who are near you. Take care of your loved ones, relatives and friends. Only together we can cope with any pandemic and survive the crisis.

I wish you all health and well-being.

# ABOUT THE AUTHOR

Mark V. Steiner is a scientist, sportsman and family person. He loves to travel, play music, spend time with his family and discover new things. If you have any questions or ideas regarding this book, you can contact Mark via his e-mail: mark.v.steiner@gmail.com